PASSIVE INCOME

A Step-By-Step Guide to Creating a Sustainable Business with Passive Income

BY

K. CONNORS

Copyright © 2017 by K. Connors

Copyright © 2017 *Passive Income* All rights reserved. No part of this publication may be reproduced, distributed, or transmitted in any form or by any means, including photocopying, recording, or other electronic or mechanical methods, without the prior written permission of the publisher, except in the case of brief quotations embodied in critical reviews and certain other noncommercial uses permitted by copyright law. This also includes conveying via e-mail without permission in writing from the publisher. All information within this book is of relevant content and written solely for motivation and direction. No financial guarantees. All information is considered valid and factual to the writer's knowledge. The author is not associated or affiliated with any company or brand mentioned in the book, therefore does not purposefully advertise nor receives payment for doing so.

Table of Contents

Introduction 1

Chapter 1: What is Passive Income 3

Chapter 2: Affiliate Marketing 7

Chapter 3: Amazon 11

Chapter 4: Freelance and Blogging 15

Chapter 5: How- To Reviews, App Creation, and Surveys 19

Chapter 6: YouTube and Social Media 23

Chapter 7: Tips and Tricks 27

INTRODUCTION

Welcome! If you are reading this book to look for a way to become financially stable without having to worry about ongoing and repetitive hours of effort, you have come to the right place. Passive income is simply a form of revenue received on a regular basis, while requiring little to no effort to maintain. This means that income is made even when you are not actively participating in the business. As of 2016 the ability to earn passive income as increased by almost three times. There are so many different outlets of achieving income as well. It is not only for the people who have a talent at crafts or are well-versed in computers. This revenue is open and available to all those who want to achieve it. We all have one life, and it is our choice on how to live it. Having a passive income gives a person the ability to not only achieve financial goals but achieve personal goals in and outside of the business.

Life is waiting for you, and from this book will be options and explanations on how to live your life, and "work" without worry. We will discuss the importance of affiliate marketing and how to find the right affiliates for you. There will be an entire chapter dedicated to Amazon.com and the resources for income provided on this site alone. We will also discuss how to use blogging and social media as a form of revenue. Also, we will discuss how to maintain a constant schedule even when your life may be hectic - through having a virtual assistant. In this book, the final chapter will discuss the importance of forums and how to make fewer mistakes when starting something new. Please note that while I list in this book many ways to make passive income, there are still many more out there. One of the most popular and my favorite is investing in real estate. For this reason, I will be releasing a new book dedicated solely to real estate investing, as it is such a large topic to cover.

CHAPTER 1

WHAT IS PASSIVE INCOME

Passive income is slowly becoming a widely-used option as a source of employment. People often create passive income with goals such as paying off student loans, making extra spending money, and even having the ability to travel the world. Now to achieve this, there will still be start-up work and a lot of patience, as learning anything new can have its ups and down. Some options may even have start-up cost, but if done correctly it may potentially turn into ten times the income in a small amount of time. When deciding on what to invest your time in for a source of passive income, it is important to look at your goals. If you want fast money, there are options such as affiliate marketing, and Amazon. However, if you want to share your experiences and adventures, there are things such as blogging, website creation, and freelance work.

What you will need:

The one thing that all of these options have in common is *a computer*. You will need a computer for work and for creating your "business." Whether it is a personal computer, family computer, or even the community computer at the library, you will need one. That is the place where people read articles, make purchases, and watch videos. So it makes sense that you will need one to make money as well.

Bank Account- If you do not have an account already, be sure to have one created as passive income online will need a place to go. They can be made in as little as twenty minutes if you walk to your nearest or most favorable bank to set one up.

PayPal Account (optional)- Though this truly is optional, it is always a great recommendation, especially if you plan on using more than one option for your income. If you have income coming from affiliate marketing, blogging, and freelancing. It can all be sent to the same place. Transferring from PayPal to your United States Bank account is always free. The reason this is recommended is because of that one dreadful word that must be said. *Taxes.* If you are using more than one site/source for your income, you will have to send in information from each and every source. From there, you must add it all up to know how much you made that year. With PayPal, however, they keep track of what comes into your PayPal account, allowing you to have all your income in one record which makes the math easy.

Business E-mail: If you have your own personal e-mail, it would not be wise to mix business with it. Making an e-mail takes only five minutes and is always free. You can choose from sites such as Yahoo, G-mail, Hotmail and several others. The only thing you will need to do is think of a business e-mail that is easy to remember and is not already taken. This will not only make you more organized but help you keep your work more professional.

Other than the things listed above, the only other thing you will need is *patience*. Starting a business from the bottom never leads to automatic success. There will be moments of planning, preparation, and waiting. Some people take months to achieve passive or even active income, while others who work diligently on their business can have fast income in weeks. The start-up cost of everything will depend on the money you are willing to spend. For example, a woman who starts a company may pay over $25,000 while another woman may spend around $200. Both of whom have the potential to be extremely successful today. This all depends on what your idea of successful is. Several of the platforms discussed in this book deal with little or no expenses, and if they do have expenses, they will usually be covered by your first paycheck. Unfortunately, sometimes you have to put forth money before you can receive it, but it will be worth it in the end.

CHAPTER 2

AFFILIATE MARKETING

The first platform for passive income is affiliate marketing. This is by far one of the cheapest, easiest, and best ways to have an income without doing anything. If you do not know what Affiliate Marketing is, it is when a website has ads and associations with other sites and products. If those products are then purchased from that site, it becomes an affiliate and receives a small portion of the income. The reason so many companies do this is because they can offer a small percentage to have their product advertised on multiple websites. So basically, being an affiliate is attaching the link to another website to your own, and if someone goes to that site and conducts a purchase from your page, you earn a percentage of that income. As a benefit for you, there is no limit to some affiliate websites you may own. Therefore, if you have three sites making a small portion of money from each, it can lead to a bigger income. The best part it, is that this is free to do. There is no before fee of advertising someone else's product. The only cost may be having someone build your website.

How to find an Affiliate-

When it comes to deciding which companies to affiliate for, it can be tough. The best advice to give is that everything needs a theme. So, when you have a website for Camping and the Outdoors, it might not be best to put links or sites related to make-up and home-décor. Find a theme that is of interest to you. If you have a hobby or passion, try to use that in your website's theme. You will know more about the topic and know what products might interest others in that area. Listed below are several vast and well-known companies that allow you to make money from home.

- **Amazon.com**
- **Nationwide Insurance**
- **American Express**
- **About.com**
- **Walmart.com**
- **IBM**
- **Nike**

The above are listed in no specific order, but are listed because almost half of the income earned from affiliate marketing came from these top sites. This is where you should put your time and effort. Notice that Amazon and Walmart are places where they have a variety of avenues allowing you to have unlimited access to products for advertising. Some websites have a questionnaire and profile that need to be created, but other than that there are no costs to using affiliate marketing as your strategy for income.

Chapter Review to-do list:

- Find a theme
- Make a website (go to bluehost.com, wordpress.com.)
- Find an affiliate
- Fill out profile
- Advertise and make money

CHAPTER 3

AMAZON

As you can see Amazon has to have its own section for the amount of income that can be given through this site. Amazon is rated #1 in all categories and in the 2016 review had taken over 37% of all online Christmas shopping. If you think about the millions of other platforms out there to buy from, that is an incredibly high percentage. Amazon is gaining its popularity due to some people using it as an affiliate, as a book-publishing ground, and as FBA. The goal of this chapter will revolve around making money solely on Amazon.

Amazon Kindle Publishing (AKP)- Kindle books and Kindle tablets have become a very popular source of reading. It makes it easier to have one object with hundreds of options than hundreds of objects on one thing. So, Amazon created a Kindle publishing platform where people can publish their works onto Amazon and create a book. Self-publishing books may not be your style, but they are a serious income booster. If you are not into writing books or don't want to spend the time on it, feel free to hire out a freelancer to write the book for you. Then, all you need to do is post it to the website and watch as people purchase and read your book, allowing you to receive royalties. It is important to make sure it is still a quality product, however, because bad reviews will lead to fewer sales of your book.

Amazon FBA (Fulfillment by Amazon)- This is where you can make more money but does come with a first purchase. Since Amazon has so many products offered to sell, it is used as a platform where other people can sell their products as well. The way you can make the most of this is by finding brand new items that are cheaper in-store and selling them through Amazon. For this, you will need to download the app called *Amazon Seller*. It is available for both iPhone and Android. It will allow you to scan barcodes in department stores to see if the item is more expensive on Amazon. If it is, then you could buy it from that store and send it to an Amazon warehouse. Once that item is purchased from Amazon, you will be the one to receive the income. Let's say you found a brand new sleeping bag at Walmart for $10. You scan the barcode, and it shows that same exact sleeping bag on Amazon. Only, it is selling for $40. Therefore, if you buy that sleeping bag and send it to an Amazon warehouse, it will stay there until someone purchases it. Once it is purchased, you will receive the $40. So, since you spent $10 to buy it, you, in turn, made $30 profit. Now, you do have to set up an Amazon Seller Account. There is no fee for the small profit sellers, but if you plan to make some significant profits, it would be recommended to do the Amazon Seller Pro which is $40 a month. To start out, you can enjoy it for free, and then eventually expand into a bigger playing field.

PASSIVE INCOME

<u>Affiliate Amazon</u>- Just like we mentioned in the previous chapter, almost anything that is sold on Amazon is available for affiliate marketing. When something is purchased from one of your websites, you will receive a small percentage of the cost of that item. Bigger priced items mean more potential income, however, remember to keep it within the theme of your website. If you have a gaming site, you will find that the Amazon links associated with gaming will sell much more than any other advertisement you may provide. The only cons noted by some users of the affiliate program is that Amazon does take a fairly high percentage. As a secret to this and since this book focuses on finding income the easy way, look at Walmart.com for the item you have in mind first. Walmart gives the affiliates more of a percentage than Amazon.

Chapter Review to-do list:

- Amazon Kindle Publishing- Computer, Word document, and freelance websites.
- Amazon FBA- Amazon Seller App and an Amazon Seller Account (amazon.com/services)

CHAPTER 4

FREELANCE AND BLOGGING

When people bring up Freelance work, many people assume that it is just strictly writing or some odd skill that takes years and years to learn. However, that is not the case. It can be anything from programming, web development, advertising, online lessons, tutorials, and more. Some people make money daily by giving shout-outs on their social media page. This is all very passive and easy work to do if you find the right thing to work with. Many of these methods you do not need previous skill to work, although it is suggested. There are even sellers out there who make hundreds of dollars a month just to send anonymous glitter. I would take a few minutes and browse the internet for some of the wacky freelance work that people actually pay for. If there is something you might be good at, people will want to buy it. Listed below will be several of the top freelancing sites as of 2016.

Top Freelancing sites:

- UpWork.com
- Elance.com

- **Freelancer.com**
- **Fiverr.com**
- **SimplyHired.com**
- **Craigslist.com**

Made it into the top ten on one of the lists. Even though you might think this site is just for buying and selling, a lot of freelance work is offered here that deals with more physical labor and delivery.

Consider each site and see which one is suited best for you, the best advice should be to find an outlet that is attractive and unique. For example, one person on Fiverr.com makes his rent payments by painting a name on his belly and shaking it for a video. As bizarre as that sounds, it is working for him. When you think you have figured out the freelance portion of it, it may be a good time to start a blog. Blog about your life, your pets, your passion, and even your trials of having passive income. When you realize how easy it is to make money, people will often try and follow in your footsteps to do the same. Starting a blog will help you maintain clients and readers, making it easier to advertise your product and freelance.

Blogging-

Blogging may sound easy to start up, but getting into it is a little harder than you think. Blogs that are successful and have a massive following are because they focus and dedicate their time into posting or hiring someone to post for them. When blogging, it is important to remember a theme as well. One popular niche is pets. If you post about pets, whether it be pet training or just adorable puppy pictures once every week, you will slowly but surely grow in followers and readers. If you want to do things completely hands-free and work free then you will need a *virtual assistant*. A virtual assistant is someone who "assists" you in the online world. You give them your profile information for your social media account, email, etc. and they will work on your page themselves with ideally positive results. This person will need to be paid a certain pre-discussed amount, but having someone run your social media accounts while you are off following your dreams is what this book strives to prepare you for.

Chapter Review To-Do list:

- Choose a freelance career (writing, editing, programming, photo taking)
- Choose a freelance site (or hire a Virtual Assistant)
- Have your website theme
- Blog and write about your theme

CHAPTER 5

HOW- TO REVIEWS, APP CREATION, AND SURVEYS

In this day and age, we have experienced both good and bad quality items. I'll go out on a limb here and say that most people today typically spend their money with caution, which is why so many people make money from doing reviews online. Whether you do reviews on your own web page or on YouTube, individuals who are money conscious will often search for reviews and recommendations before making an actual purchase. This is where you can make your passive income as well. All it takes is for you to make a review video on a product of your choosing. Specifically, something that you might have experience in or a passion for. If you enjoy fishing, consider writing reviews on a fishing pole. If you enjoy computers, then make a review of your laptop. You only have to make the video once, and it will be available to all those who search for it. The best way to make the most out of it to have all the chapter subjects combine. If you have your website, you can post your video review, and on the side of the screen can be external links to Amazon or other sites where people can click on those links and find their answers. That way, your site is making you money from all different directions.

How-To/Reviews start-up- This is a How-To on How-Tos. When it comes to making a video, there are several things to consider: light quality, sound quality, and image quality. When making videos, it is also a good idea to be honest, especially with review videos. People want to know that they can trust your judgment. There are several different channels dedicated to only reviews, and they gain subscribers by the day. If you can find a subject such as cooking utensils, paint, gadgets, or more, you will find that doing reviews may be easy and fun at the same time. Doing reviews online is something that will more than likely not fall in popularity as more and more people are becoming more conscious about spending money and will research as much as possible. Throwing in a little comedy here and there will always help as well.

App Creation- If you are a programmer or designer, this could be an incredible opportunity for you. App creation can reach millions of people quickly, and continue to earn money worldwide. However, do not stress if your computer skills are sub-par or below. It is just as easy to outsource the work. Living without having to worry about work is part of the outsourcing. If you can outsource someone to create the app, then you are the one getting the money for it passively. You literally did nothing but hire the help and are still able to earn an income (assuming you have a killer unique app idea of course). Programming is also a big money maker when you can produce a good quality product or service. Finding and app niche is the next step. Once you have found what you think is a profitable niche, you can outsource, and then upload. There are several different ways to make money off an app; the top two are having the app be a Paid App, in the Android and iPhone store, or by having in-app purchases. Those two ways are how you can make the most of your passive income. The more your app has to offer, the more likely it is to be downloaded and used. It does not have to be a game app; it can be a productive app, an app dealing with business or even an app with recipes. Everyone has different interests, and someone out there is looking for an app that you might just be the answer for.

Surveys- As much as you may think it sounds cheesy, it is shockingly simple and really can give you a fair passive income. Some of these survey sites are not only filling out surveys, but product testing as well. This is where a lot of revenue comes into play. Start-up businesses or other product creators who need reviews and feedback will often give you free supplies or pay for your response. This will not only earn you an income, but you may get some free product as well. There are hundreds of survey sites out there, however, and unfortunately, some of them are false. However, if you find the right survey site, you could be making anywhere from $3-$40 dollars a day. If you do that on your free time while having a website and affiliate group, you should no problem in producing a passive income.

Things a real survey site will NOT ask:

- **Your card information**

- To pay a "fee."
- Bank information

All survey sites should be completely free to use as well as simple. None of them will ask for your bank information either, they all should be directly associated with PayPal. Surveys are also something that accumulates with points. Making points could be as easy or as hard as the site wants it to be. Though it does make you money, it may also be a little bit of a waiting game as well. Several people use this as their only source of income, though they take surveys and test products as well. Be sure to double check the legitimacy of the website before nosediving right into it.

Chapter Review To-Do list:

- Find something to review
- Make a video
- PayPal account
- Survey sites

CHAPTER 6

YOUTUBE AND SOCIAL MEDIA

Social media is everywhere, and it is steadily growing as the websites evolve and motivate their audiences. That is why so many people are making money from their accounts, and the good news is that there are several platforms from which to work. Sites like Twitter, Facebook, Instagram, and of course YouTube. The reason people can earn an income from this is through persistence and perseverance. This is a long term income but also takes a long time to fulfill. The amount of follows and subscribers will depend on your activity. If you socialize and maintain a relationship with your followers, you are more likely to gain them much quicker than if you were to not. If you are not as free with your time, it may be relatively hard to maintain a decent income from this. When it comes to YouTube, however, there are a few different platforms you can take. YouTube does not pay you for the subscribers; it pays you for the views. If your video gets more than 50k views, you can start earning a small paycheck, the more viral the videos, the more income.

Virtual Assistant-

As silly as it sounds, people prefer to hire a virtual assistant for their social media accounts because it is much simpler and they can live their life with someone else doing the social media work for them. As strange as it sounds, this is the case for most celebrities. They do not have time to keep an active ongoing social media site and tend to pay someone to do the work for them instead. Having a virtual assistant on an account can be a permanent or temporary thing to keep your followers increasing and your product promoted.

How to get to the top-

Unfortunately, there is no short way of cutting to the top. Many people tend to buy followers or try to cheat to be popular, but YouTube, Twitter, and Instagram have a very strict terms and agreement policy which can lead to removing content or even being banned. If you really want to make it big in social media, it will require a lot of patience.

YouTube- Making YouTube videos have been a popular source of income for many, and it has surpassed longer than many thought it would. YouTube is the number one tutorial site as well as one of the most visited sites behind Google. There will always be a platform here that can help you obtain your goals, as long as you are willing to work hard. If you have a hobby or passion, film it and share it. People often enjoy living through virtual reality when they are unable or unwilling to do it themselves. Vlogging has become increasingly popular as more and more people begin filming their daily lives. Yes, that's Vlogging with a V. If you are interested in sharing your life with the world, people will watch. You will be able to make money by literally living day by day. The equipment you will need for it will vary depending on your idea. A video camera of course, though many people just tend just to use their cellphone cameras since the video and sound quality is always improving. The best part is that if you are unable to edit the video, you can easily find hundreds of freelancers that are ready and willing to do it for you. The only cost would be for the edits, and you will be able to promote and encourage views with other virtual assistants.

To ensure that your video will be of high quality and good content, it may prove useful to have someone do the editing and promoting for you, if that is not a strong suit of yours. If you do a below average job on editing and sound quality, it will not gather as many views. Make sure your product is quality.

Chapter Review to-do list:

- Decide on your social media platform
- Hire Virtual Assistant

CHAPTER 7

TIPS AND TRICKS

In this book, we discussed the importance of patience and hard work; however, this may not even be the most important thing to have. The most significant are resources. If you can attain and achieve multiple resources, you will have an easier and more solid chance with passive income. Whatever social media site you may use, there will be groups relating to your idea line of work. If you want to freelance you can be sure that there will be hundreds of groups from which to choose. This is the same with programming, advertising, or even blogging. The reason finding groups is so important is that it avoids making mistakes that have already been answered. People are already making money on the platform you chose. They have already made errors that needed to be learned from and have failed and tried until they succeeded. Since these groups are there for free and for the taking, you may be better off joining one to make sure you become as successful as possible. Read the questions that are asked and answered; if you have a question, feel free to ask it. ASK QUESTIONS that you may have instead of trying to figure it out on your own every time. Everyone involved in the group has been where you are right now, and they won't leave you hanging so that you can fail. They will help you to the best of their ability so you can avoid the mistakes they have already made.

Be social- if someone within your group is having trouble, feel free to respond or look at the comments already answered. You may find that you learn something you did not know before. If you are on a freelance site, feel free to use the blogs and forums provided by that site. They are all there specifically for the sellers as a tool for making the work easier and more profitable. It especially helps if the website itself is having problems, because this will be something typically only the website forums can answer.

Take a chance- If you can spend a little towards your passive income, it may be the little push you need to start. Do something you normally wouldn't do; try out the freelance opportunities and you may find that you like writing for others or working as someone else's virtual assistant. The freelance opportunities are endless, but you will be more successful if you can expand your abilities and options.

Make sure you are patient. I bring that to light again as it does take at least a month or two of hard work before anything is completely passive. Passive income is the new way to make money and will always be available; it is up to you to take the chance and achieve it. You can do it; anyone can do it. Just by reading this book you are already a few steps closer to reaching an income and knowing where to start and what to do.

You have learned about what passive income is, and several different places from which to achieve it. We discussed the importance of affiliate marketing and where to find the right fit for you. We explained the simplicity and ease of working with Amazon and how there are several different opportunities within just one site. Whether you want to write and publish books, sell a physical product, or even become their affiliate advertiser, there are endless opportunities out there. I also tried to explain the importance and wide range of niches in the freelancing department. Showing you that there is income in that direction too. You just need to find that one subject that will make you the most successful. Blogging and surveys are another form of income that can be achieved in as little as ten minutes. If there is a time to start your passive income it is right now. There is no time like the present! This moment will not come again, and you do not want to miss the opportunity to take control of your life and live how you want to live, not by the hours on a time sheet.

Chapter review to-do list:

- Find forums
- Find Facebook/ social media pages relating to your niche
- Ask questions
- Be patient

** Thank you very much for sharing an interest in my book. As a writer, I work hard to create and bring accurate, relative content to my readers. If you enjoyed this book, please leave a review on Amazon. If you have any questions, concerns, or criticism, please feel free to email me directly at kconnorsbooks@gmail.com. **

Printed in Great Britain
by Amazon